REVIEW COPY
COURTESY OF
ENSLOW PUBLISHERS, INC.

Other titles in the  **series:**

Investigate
Alcohol

Library ISBN: 978-0-7660-4235-7

Paperback ISBN: 978-1-4644-0449-8

Investigate
Club Drugs

Library ISBN: 978-0-7660-4221-6

Paperback ISBN: 978-1-4644-0385-9

Investigate
Cocaine and Crack

Library ISBN: 978-0-7660-4255-1

Paperback ISBN: 978-1-4644-0453-5

Investigate
Methamphetamine

Library ISBN: 978-0-7660-4254-4

Paperback ISBN: 978-1-4644-0451-1

Investigate
Steroids and Performance Drugs

Library ISBN: 978-0-7660-4240-7

Paperback ISBN: 978-1-4644-0423-8

INVESTIGATE
Club Drugs

INVESTIGATE

DRUGS

**Alison and Stephen
Eldridge**

E **Enslow Publishers, Inc.**
40 Industrial Road
Box 398
Berkeley Heights, NJ 07922
USA

http://www.enslow.com

Library of Congress Cataloging-in-Publication Data

Eldridge, Alison.
    Investigate club drugs / by Alison and Stephen Eldridge.
      pages cm. — (Investigate drugs)
    Includes bibliographical references and index.
    Summary: "Find out what club drugs are, what happens when someone becomes
addicted, and how the addiction is treated"—Provided by publisher.
    ISBN 978-0-7660-4221-6
    1. Hallucinogenic drugs—Social aspects—Juvenile literature. 2. Psychotropic drugs—
Social aspects—Juvenile literature. I. Eldridge, Stephen. II. Title.
    HV5822.H25E43 2015
    362.29'9—dc23
                 2013009721

Future editions:
Paperback ISBN: 978-1-4644-0385-9   Single-User PDF ISBN: 978-1-4646-1212-1
EPUB ISBN: 978-1-4645-1212-4   Multi-User PDF ISBN: 978-0-7660-5844-6

052014 Lake Book Manufacturing, Inc., Melrose Park, IL
Printed in the United States of America
10 9 8 7 6 5 4 3 2 1

To Our Readers: We have done our best to make sure all Internet Addresses in this book were active and appropriate when we went to press. However, the author and the publisher have no control over and assume no liability for the material available on those Internet sites or on other Web sites they may link to. Any comments can be sent to comments@enslow.com or to the address on the back cover.

♻ Enslow Publishers, Inc., is committed to printing our books on recycled paper. The paper in every book contains 10% to 30% post-consumer waste (PCW). The cover board on the outside of each book contains 100% PCW. Our goal is to do our part to help young people and the environment too!

Photo Credits: ©Incite Productions, LLC, p. 41; ©iStockphoto.com/asiseeit, p. 89; © iStockphoto. com/Rapid Eye, pp. 74–75; Philippe Garo /Science Source, p. 59; Psychonaught/Wikipedia.com Public Domain image, p. 33; Shutterstock.com: Irina Rogova, p. 4; Anteromite, pp. 7, 17, 29, 40, 55, 70, 81; David Orcea, p. 12; Monkey Business Images, p. 15; Rob Marmion, p. 22; Andrea Danti, pp. 24–25; Emilia Ungur, p. 35; antoshkaforever, pp. 38, 53, 67, 78; Africa Studio, 45; Konstantin Sutyagin, pp. 62–63; © Thinkstock: Andersen Ross/Blend Images, p.82; Catherine Yeulet/iStock, pp. 50–51; JupiterImages/Photos. com, p.72; leviticus/iStock, p.18; neolamprologus/iStock, p.11; omgimages /iStock, pp. 84–85.

Cover Photo: Shutterstock.com/ hxdbzxy

Contents

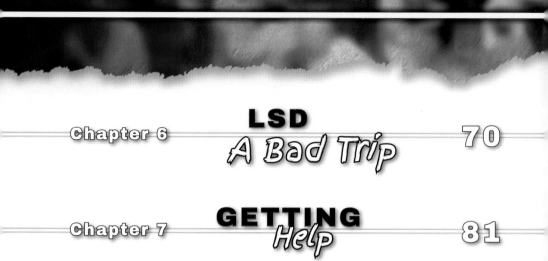

Chapter 1

DANGER
in the Club

You're with your friends, or maybe you're making new friends. There's music, there's dancing, or perhaps there's just a few people together having a good time. Eventually, someone who seems cool hands you a tab, or a powder, or even just a drink, and tells you it'll make you feel awesome. Now, you're not stupid—you know enough not to stick a needle in your arm in an alley. You've seen the movies, you know that doesn't end well. But this is a friend offering you a little fun. It's not the same thing, right?

Not so fast. Do you even know what you're being given? Does your friend? Do you know what it's been cut with— what other substances have been put in it? Do you know if it's really what you've been told it is? Do you even know

what methamphetamine, or MDMA, or Rohypnol are? Do you know what's been put in that drink?

Just because you're having fun doesn't mean you're not in danger. It's easy to feel safe when you're with your friends, but the fact is that there are always risks, and you need to be aware of them to stay safe.

In this book, you'll learn about some of the most common drugs that are used at clubs and parties. You'll read stories about people who used and abused those drugs, sometimes with deadly consequences. And you'll be given the information you need to make the right decisions—the decisions that can keep a good time from becoming a disaster—for you, your friends, and your family.

Stories of Club Drug Abuse

This book will use real-life stories of people who abused club drugs to teach you about those drugs, their effects, and their risks. These stories aren't a lot of fun—but maybe they can help you or your friends avoid the mistakes that other people have made.

In Chapter Two, you'll hear Joe's story. Joe used a drug called MDMA, which is more commonly known as "ecstasy." Ecstasy is a common party drug that looks cute on the outside but can be deadly on the inside. Your friends may tell you it will make you feel good, but that experience can come at a very high price—as Joe found out.

In Chapter Three, you'll read about Louise, a young woman who made the mistake of abusing ketamine. Ketamine is a drug that's often used in medicine to numb people before they go into surgery, or as a tranquilizer for

Past-Year Use of Illicit Drugs and Pharmaceuticals among 12th Graders

Drug	Percentage
Marijuana/Hashish	36.4%
Synthetic Marijuana	11.3%
Adderall	7.6%
Vicodin	7.5%
Cough Medicine	5.6%
Tranquilizers	5.3%
Hallucinogens	4.8%
Sedatives*	4.5%
Salvia	4.4%
OxyContin	4.3%
MDMA (Ecstasy)	3.8%
Inhalants	2.9%
Cocaine (any form)	2.7%
Ritalin	2.6%

■ Illicit Drugs

▩ Pharmaceutical

SOURCE: University of Michigan, 2012 Monitoring the Future Study

Statistics from a study in 2012 show the previous year's drug use among twelfth graders.

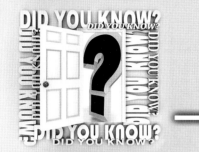

PEER
Pressure

It can be tough to be the guy or girl who says "no" while your friends are doing something, even when that thing is as dangerous as drug use. When you feel pressure to do something you don't really want to do because friends or other people your age are doing it, that's called peer pressure. Almost everyone feels peer pressure at some point, even adults, and it's important to understand how to deal with it. Remember, your decisions are your decisions—your friends don't get to decide for you.

Be prepared to say no, even if it upsets people. Most of the time, it won't. You can even practice on your own with friends so you feel confident saying no. "No, thanks, I'm not into that" is a simple and firm reply. People who offer you drugs will just shrug and move on if you turn them down. Give your friends a little credit. They'll get over any annoyance or disappointment. Being afraid to upset your friends isn't a good reason to take a risk you don't want to take. Occasionally, people might be mean about it. But do you really want to be friends with people like that?

Remember, whenever drugs and alcohol are involved, there's risk. You're going to have to make decisions that could be the difference between life and death. Being a little uncomfortable for a few minutes when you tell someone "no" is a small price to pay for being safe. And when you say no, you might be taking the pressure off someone else—if they see that it's okay for you to be different, they might feel like it's okay for them to be different, too. Resisting peer pressure isn't just standing up for yourself, it can be a way of standing up for your friends, too.[1]

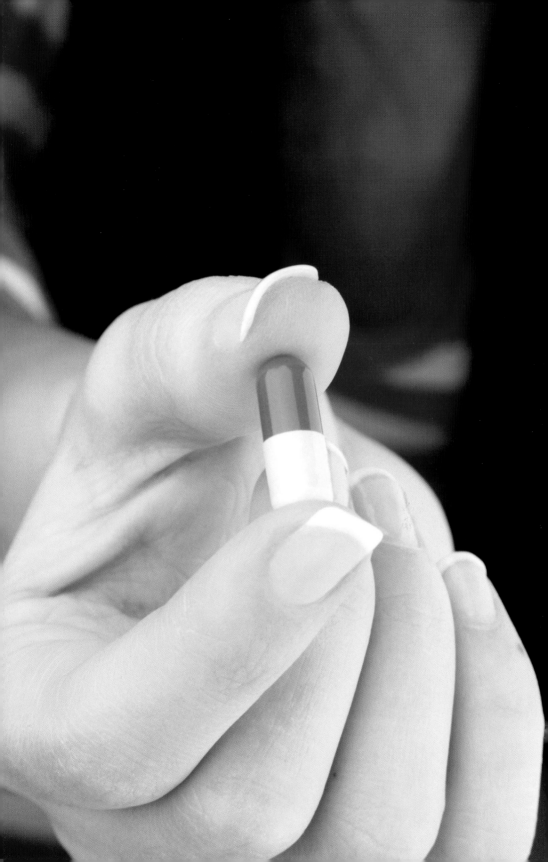

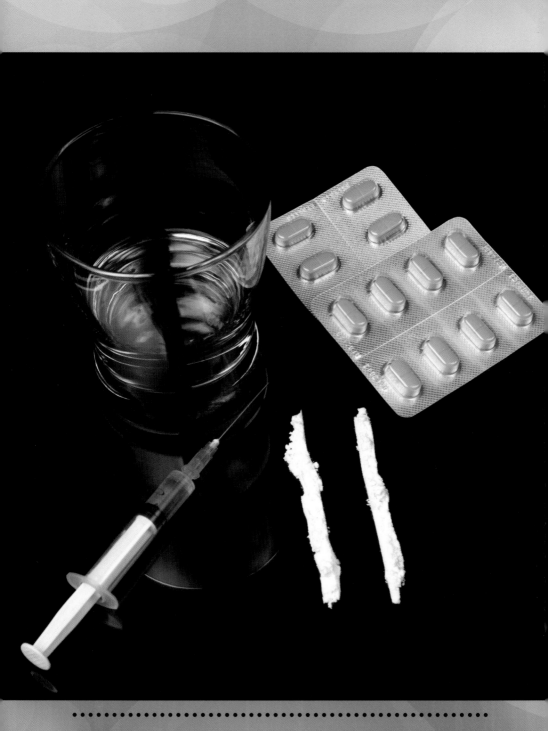

Any pill, powder, or liquid has the potential to be dangerous.

animals. Some people think that because ketamine can be used by doctors it can't be that bad. Unfortunately for Louise, that isn't true.

In Chapter Four, you'll be introduced to Carren, a young woman who tried to escape her troubles by using methamphetamine, or "crystal meth." Crystal meth is one of the most dangerous and addictive drugs in the world. Instead of helping Carren escape her problems, it gave her a whole lot of new ones.

In Chapter Five, you'll hear the story of Heather, a girl who was dosed with Rohypnol. Rohypnol and other drugs, such as GHB, are often given to people secretly in drinks. The victims are then abused or otherwise taken advantage of. Heather didn't suspect that someone might be trying to hurt her, but you don't have to be caught unawares for these drugs to be harmful.

In Chapter Six, you'll find out about Timothy Castaneda, who got caught up abusing LSD, also called "acid." LSD makes people have strange, vivid hallucinations—they see visions or hear sounds that aren't really there. As Timothy learned, just because those hallucinations aren't real doesn't mean LSD can't hurt you.

What You Need to Know

The most important thing you'll learn from this book is how to protect yourself from these harmful drugs. The most important thing to remember is that any pill, powder, or liquid you're given is potentially dangerous. Even if you're just trying it, the purpose of every drug mentioned in this book is to somehow make you act in ways you wouldn't

THE NUMBER ONE CLUB DRUG: *Alcohol*

No book on club drugs would be complete without a little information about the most common club drug of all: alcohol. People usually don't think of alcohol as a drug, because it's (mostly) legal and because so many people use it. But alcohol is a drug, and it can be as dangerous as any of the drugs listed in this book.

Abuse of alcohol is a serious problem. Binge drinking is when you drink a lot in a short period of time, especially when you do it regularly. Binge drinking can damage your brain, your liver, and your heart—and you need all of those to survive! Even if you don't binge drink often, too much alcohol at once can give you alcohol poisoning, which is potentially deadly. And, of course, no one should ever drive after drinking. Drunk and "buzzed" drivers kill thousands of people every year—often themselves, their friends, or their families.

It's especially easy for young people to misjudge their limits. They usually have a lower tolerance for alcohol and don't have much experience with it. It's best for everyone if teens wait until the legal age to use alcohol, and do it in a safe environment with people who they trust to help them if they make a mistake.

As dangerous as alcohol can be on its own, it becomes even more so when other drugs get involved. Reactions between alcohol and other drugs can make you sick. Adding the effects of alcohol can make other drugs more powerful and their risks much higher. Drinking can even make you more vulnerable to being drugged by someone else—if alcohol is already messing up your mind, you might not notice the effects of another drug until it's too late.[2]

normally act. Maybe you'll be too high to behave normally and you will hurt yourself. Maybe the drug will mess with your heart or your brain and do damage to your body. Maybe you'll feel so different that you'll do something you shouldn't and become infected with a disease, or hurt in a car crash. Or maybe not—maybe you'll be lucky the first time, or the second, or the third, and only later find out what kind of damage you've been doing to yourself. Either way, you need to know the risks to make the right decisions.

Sometimes it's not as easy as just saying "no." Unfortunately, any time you go to a club or party you could be a target for people who will try to take advantage of you. The best way to stay safe is to make sure that you don't accept drinks from people you don't know very well—or, better yet, only drink things you've gotten yourself. It's also important to stay around close friends. Make sure that you and your friends watch out for each other. If someone is acting strangely, it could be that they've been drugged and need help.

Remember, there's nothing wrong with having fun—but not if someone gets hurt.

Chapter 2

MDMA/ECSTASY
A Night Out Turns Deadly

Sixteen-year-old Joe Simons and his friends counted themselves pretty lucky when they were let into a Bristol, England, nightclub on April 30, 2011, without having to show any ID. The four teens had decided to head to the club for a night of fun—and a bit of MDMA, a drug commonly known on the street as ecstasy. After doing some research on the Internet they had given the drug a try the month before at the same club. What they found made them think ecstasy would be a "safe" choice for a good time. It's supposed to make you loving and energetic. And, unlike "hard" drugs such as heroin, it's not especially addictive. The first time, they were lucky. They thought it would be "safe" this time, too.

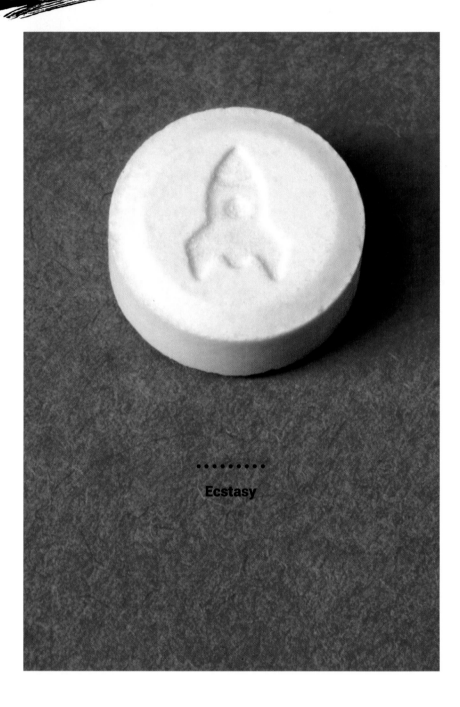

Ecstasy

Joe was a bright young man who got good grades in school. He hoped to go to either Oxford or Cambridge, England's top universities. He was also an athlete in excellent shape and played hockey, cricket, and rugby at school. But even smarts and good health weren't enough to keep Joe from making a big mistake.[1]

Inside the club Joe easily found a dealer who sold him 1.5 grams of powdered MDMA. He split it with his friends, and they all took it with water. A short time later, Joe's friends noticed his skin was turning grey and he was staring off into the distance. He couldn't stand up without being supported.[2] Eventually he was laid down on the floor of the club. Joe was rushed to a hospital but died early the next morning of multiple organ failure.[3] Although Joe Simons was found to have taken more than four times the amount of MDMA people usually take, this drug can be dangerous even in small amounts.

Methyl-who?

The full scientific name of the drug known as MDMA is 3,4-methylenedioxymethamphetamine—no wonder it goes by so many nicknames! It was first developed in the early 1900s as an appetite suppressant (a drug that makes people feel less hungry), but it wasn't officially approved for this use. It later became a popular drug in psychotherapy. By the 1980s, MDMA was mostly being used for fun at parties. These parties, often called "raves," were centered around drug use, electronic music, and dancing. They were especially popular in the United Kingdom.[4] Over the following years

MDMA's popularity spread to other countries and it started to appear frequently at nightclubs as well.

In 1985, MDMA was added to the international Convention on Psychotropic Substances, a United Nations treaty drawn up to help control the spread of dangerous drugs. The United Nations is a worldwide organization that discusses and makes laws about global issues. The treaty made MDMA illegal worldwide, although different countries make their own laws and decide how to enforce them. It became illegal in the United States in 1988. However, millions of people still make, sell, and use MDMA illegally. In the United States a first-time offender can get up to ten years in prison for being caught with just 25 grams of the stuff.

Most of the MDMA sold in the United States is made in laboratories in Canada and Europe and smuggled into the country. From 2006 to 2010, the amount of MDMA seized by law enforcement officials at the Canadian border doubled from 500 pounds to 1,000 pounds. Getting caught smuggling the drug into the country is also a serious offense. It can land you in jail for 20 years!

Deceiving Looks

MDMA is often sold in powder form, but more often it's sold pressed into pills. Lots of times these pills are in cute shapes, like cartoon characters, or they're stamped with fun symbols like lightning bolts, zodiac signs, or butterflies to make them seem more appealing. Especially in this case, looks can be deceiving.[5] People will tell you ecstasy will make you feel warm and fuzzy, and more loving toward others. It may make you feel like you're drunk and heighten sensations, especially touch. You may become more energetic. These are some of the reasons MDMA is popular in clubs where people are dancing to loud music under flashing lights. Some people say it will make you feel more spiritually enlightened. People may even try to convince you that ecstasy is a "safe" drug and that it won't cause harm or addiction.

What people won't tell you is that MDMA can have a lot of unpleasant side effects. Some of them can be really dangerous, even deadly. While this drug may make you feel close to your friends, it's heightening your emotions all around. This can lead to increased anxiety and panic attacks—episodes in which you feel extremely scared and may act out of control. MDMA may also make you clench your jaw and grind your teeth, have muscle spasms, or vomit. You may get chills and sweat a lot or get cramps in your legs. Your vision may get blurry as your blood pressure rises and your heart rate increases. And when it's all over many people feel much worse than they did before, uncontrollably depressed and upset.

The more you take, the more dangerous it becomes. And, as with Joe Simons, there's always the risk of death, no matter how many times you've tried it. Taking too much MDMA can make you dangerously dehydrated. It can interfere with your body's ability to control its temperature. If you get too overheated, a condition called hyperthermia, your organs may start to fail. MDMA can also tamper with your heart's ability to pump blood normally. These effects are especially dangerous in a nightclub setting, where the

MDMA may raise your blood pressure.

drug will make you want to dance and lose track of yourself. It's very easy to become dehydrated and overtired from all that energy and sensory overload. If you aren't treated quickly for these conditions, you may die.[6]

This Is Your Brain on Drugs

So how does MDMA make you feel the way it does? The answer is in how your brain functions. Nerve cells in your brain called neurons send and receive messages to help your brain function. You have billions of these cells working all the time. They communicate by sending chemicals called neurotransmitters to each other. There are many different types of neurotransmitters, and they have different functions. MDMA increases the function of three of these: serotonin, which regulates things like emotion, sleep, and pain response; dopamine, which controls the brain's reward and pleasure centers as well as your ability to pay attention; and norepinephrine, which controls the body's fight-or-flight response and can make you feel anxious and increase your heart rate. MDMA most heavily affects serotonin, causing a lot of it to be released at once. This is what causes your heightened emotions and sensations. It also makes you feel happier and closer to others. MDMA can be injected, snorted, or taken by mouth. The time that it takes for the effects to be felt depends on how the drug was taken. These effects can last three to six hours.[7]

While the "favorable" results of MDMA may last for hours, the side effects can last for days—or maybe forever. Eventually your neurons start running out of serotonin to release. This is when you "crash" and start to feel irritable

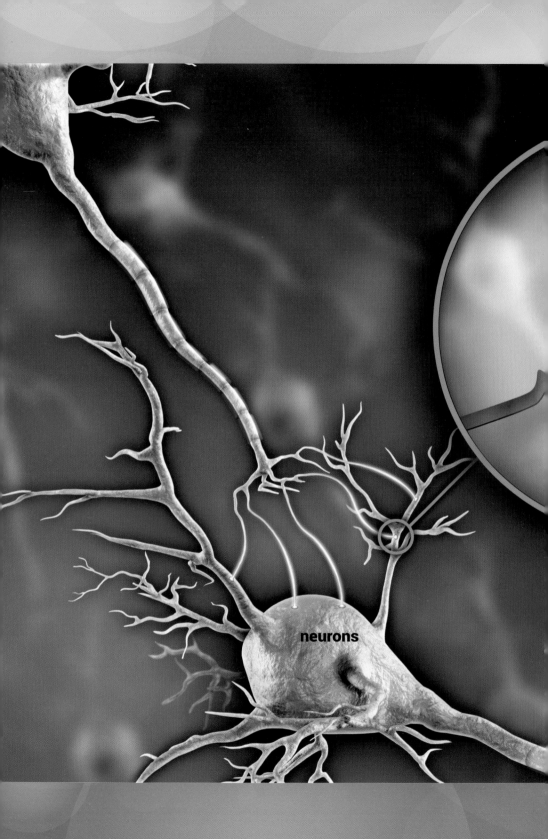

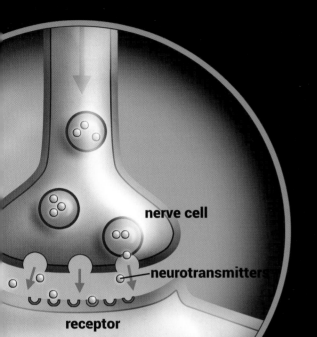

nerve cell

neurotransmitters

receptor

Neurons in your brain send and receive signals through neurotransmitters. MDMA increases the function of three neurotransmitters that affect many body functions, such as pleasure, heart rate, and pain.

and depressed. Many people, when they start to feel this way, try to take another dose of ecstasy to feel normal again. But it takes your brain a while to replenish your supply of serotonin, and the next dose may not work at all. Eventually you can completely use up your serotonin, and you may be depressed for weeks afterward.

To make matters worse, studies have shown that this overuse of serotonin can cause brain damage that leads to memory loss or chronic depression. It can also affect the appetite and ability to sleep. The more you take MDMA, the more your body becomes used to its effects. That means you'll have to take more and more just to feel anything.

When You Can't Stop

Studies show that many people continue to use MDMA despite knowing that it is dangerous or having experienced dangerous effects, and that use can lead to withdrawal symptoms. Signs of withdrawal include depression, fatigue, loss of appetite, and inability to concentrate. Also, it can affect the reward centers of the brain. Addictive drugs trick the brain into thinking they are good for the body by activating these centers. This is good evidence that MDMA can be addictive.

Once you are addicted to a drug, you will find it difficult to stop taking it. You may think that you could stop at any time, but continue to use it even when it becomes a danger to your health. Addicts will often do anything to get their hands on their drug of choice, including lying and stealing. They obsessively think about when and where they will get their next dose.

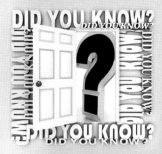

WHAT'S IN
This Stuff?

The side effects of MDMA can be really scary, but using this drug can be even scarier. A lot of times, in order to make MDMA cheaper to manufacture or more addictive, people will combine it with other substances. Sometimes these other substances are illegal drugs, such as methamphetamine (see Chapter Four) or cocaine. Sometimes they're drugs that are available over the counter, like aspirin, caffeine, or dextromethorphan (a cough suppressant).

Any of these drugs can be dangerous in high doses, and many of them can react poorly with MDMA or worsen its side effects. Recently, MDMA tablets have been found to be mixed with a drug called "bath salts" that causes a much stronger high—and a much stronger comedown, too. Bath salts have been in the news a lot for making people suddenly and uncontrollably violent to themselves and others. They make users hallucinate and lose control. If you think that's bad, drug dealers will sometimes try to trick buyers by selling them pills that don't have any MDMA in them at all. These pills could be made of anything, and that means it's impossible to know what the risks of taking them might be.

If you are afraid that you or a friend may be addicted to MDMA, you should seek help immediately. Tell a trustworthy adult about your or your friend's drug use. Treatment for MDMA addiction includes using medications to help withdrawal symptoms and therapy to learn how to stop cravings. With help you can conquer your addiction before it conquers you.

Chapter 3

KETAMINE,
Bad Medicine

Louise Cattell had the kind of life most people would envy. Louise lived in one of the world's great cities with her best friend as a roommate. At 21, the pretty Londoner was already a talented photographer and DJ and had recently applied to art college. She had helped to organize London Fashion Week, and had even appeared on the popular talent show *The X Factor*. She loved to have fun—and unfortunately "fun" sometimes included a drug called ketamine.

Louise had just dropped off her portfolio at the art school she hoped to attend. She and her roommate decided to have some friends over for dinner. They had a nice meal (cooking was another of Louise's many talents), and drank some wine. Louise and some of her friends also took some ketamine. Ketamine is probably most well-known as a horse tranquilizer, but sometimes people use it to get high. Louise and her friends snorted ketamine and watched some television.

Louise's roommate decided to go to bed. Louise was tired, but felt restless and decided a bath might help her relax. Unfortunately, she was right. Louise fell asleep in the tub and sank beneath the water. Under the influence of ketamine, she couldn't wake up despite the water filling her lungs. Louise drowned, unable to save herself because of the drug she had taken.

Louise's roommate found her dead in the bath the next morning. She called for help, but it was too late to save her friend.

Hundreds of people came to mourn Louise at her funeral. Her grief-stricken parents had wanted to have a private funeral, but the sheer number of people hurt by Louise's death demanded otherwise. A single bad decision not only cost Louise her life, but hurt the many people who had known and loved her. All that pain can be traced back to abuse of the drug ketamine.

It might be tempting to view this tragedy as exceptional because Louise Cattell was an exceptional person. But there's nothing unusual about ketamine abuse, which has become shockingly common at clubs and parties. Unfortunately, people get the idea that it has no risks or side effects. That can be a fatal mistake.[1,2]

Louise Cattell was an ambitious young woman who had helped organize London Fashion Week.

Keta-who?

Like many drugs, ketamine isn't just taken illegally. Ketamine has legal medical uses. It was originally developed as an anesthetic—a drug that can numb people's pain during surgery or other medical care. Ketamine can make you feel numb all over, or make it seem like your mind is separate from your body (an effect called dissociation). A high enough dose can knock you out entirely. Maybe the most famous use for ketamine isn't on people at all, though—it's used as a tranquilizer for horses and other animals.

But just because ketamine has medical uses doesn't mean it's safe. Drugs doctors use can be just as dangerous as street drugs. In the case of ketamine, anesthesiologists are trained to administer the right dose in controlled circumstances to get the desired effect. Too much can cause serious problems. They also often combine ketamine with drugs that make it less dangerous—alone, ketamine can cause seizures.

Remember, ketamine is legal for doctors to prescribe, but you can still get in trouble for having it illegally. Possession of ketamine without a prescription can get you up to three years in jail, or a $250,000 fine.

Abusing Ketamine

So why would anyone use ketamine, anyway? At low doses, some users experience a pleasant, "dream-like" state or a feeling of floating. It can cause hallucinations, including the dissociative effect mentioned above. Unlike some other

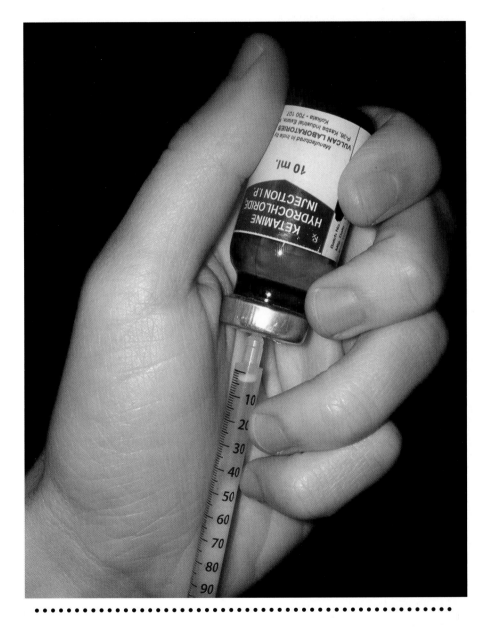

Ketamine is a prescription drug used as an anesthetic and also as an animal tranquilizer.

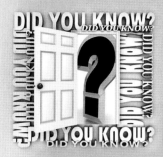

KETAMINE'S A
Real Downer

You may have heard the terms "upper" or "downer" when people talk about drugs. This doesn't mean uppers are good and downers are bad; it just tells you what the effects of the drugs are. Uppers are stimulants—drugs that make you feel more awake or alert and may make you feel like you have lots of energy. Downers are depressants. Depressants don't necessarily make you feel sad, they just make you feel more relaxed, less alert, or tired.

Both stimulants and depressants can be dangerous, especially when mixed together. Ketamine is a very powerful depressant and should only be mixed with other drugs by trained doctors. Unfortunately, many people who use ketamine illegally don't take this advice.

One of the most common depressants out there is actually legal: alcohol. Although in small amounts alcohol is a stimulant, in larger amounts it is a depressant. Alcohol reduces your body's ability to work correctly. Like ketamine, it makes you less alert and can slow you down. When alcohol and ketamine are taken together, the combined effect of both downers can be dangerous—even deadly.

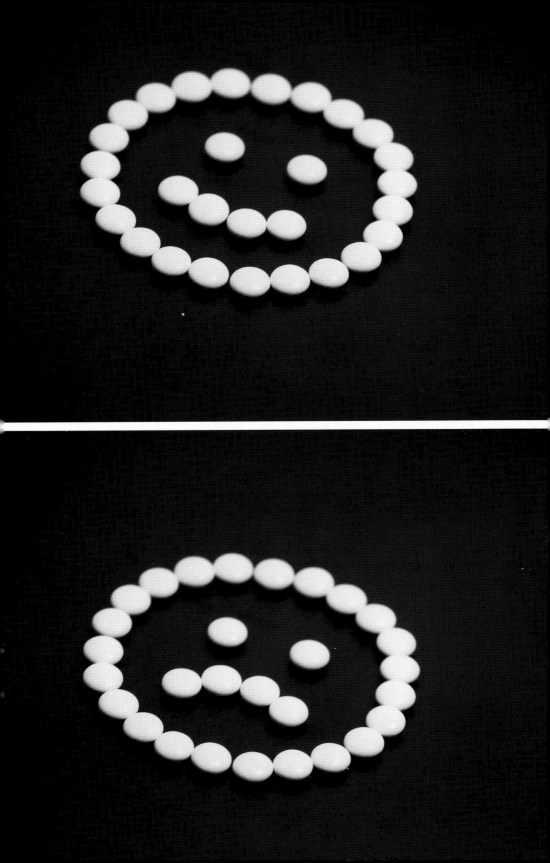

drugs, the major effects of ketamine usually wear off within a couple of hours. Some people think it's a fun experience.

What they don't usually think about are the side effects. Aside from seizures, ketamine can cause a wide variety of side effects. Some of them are short-term: high blood pressure, nausea, dizziness, confusion, racing heartbeat, memory loss, and more. Some of these are unpleasant, others are dangerous.

One of the most common side effects is known as the "K-hole." This is like the "bad trip" you might get from other hallucinogens. People who experience the K-hole feel so far detached from their bodies that they may feel like they're dead or dying. The experience is terrifying, but there's no way to stop it until the drug wears off.

Even worse? The side effects from long-term use. Usually doctors don't worry too much about long-term effects, because people are only given ketamine very rarely. However, people who abuse ketamine can have all kinds of problems. Some of them include depression, permanent memory loss, delusions, and incontinence—that is, people who use too much ketamine may start peeing their pants.[3]

Of course, maybe the most dangerous thing about ketamine is how it affects your mind. The dissociative effects of the drug can make it difficult to understand what's happening to you—even when it's dangerous. You can seriously hurt yourself and not even know it until you wake up in the hospital. Or, like Louise, you can end up putting yourself in mortal danger and be unable to save yourself.[4]

When You Can't Stop

Like many drugs, you can build a resistance to ketamine, meaning you need more and more of it to get the same effect. It's also psychologically addictive—people who use ketamine often think they need to use it again and again. This leads to people using too much too often, which can make all the side effects worse. Regular ketamine use can be a danger to your body and your mind. If you suspect you or a friend may be addicted to ketamine, get help from a trustworthy adult.

How to Identify—and Avoid—Ketamine

Because it's very difficult to make, almost all ketamine comes from medical sources. Ketamine made for medicinal purposes is liquid. Sometimes this liquid is smoked, or added to other drugs that are smoked. However, it is usually sold illegally as a powder. In its liquid form, ketamine is clear, or slightly cloudy. To get a powder, the liquid drug is spread out and left to dry. It usually forms small crystal shards as it dries. The crystals are ground into a fine white powder that can be hard to tell from other drugs, like cocaine or GHB. Sometimes the drug ends up in larger bits that might look like coarse salt. It's then usually eaten or snorted. It can even be injected with a needle.

Like other drugs, ketamine can be especially dangerous because of other substances mixed in with it. These substances range from unpleasant—like table salt—to deadly—like other medicines and drugs that can react

THE NAME
Game

Like most drugs, ketamine has a lot of street names. Some of them are pretty obvious—if someone offers you "Ket" or "K," you can probably figure out that you should turn them down. If you hear that "Special K" is going around at a party, it's probably not cereal. "Vitamin K" is a real vitamin your body needs, but unless you bought it from the supermarket, it's probably not good for you.

Some names are a little more creative. "Donkey dust" is a reference to the fact that ketamine is used as an animal tranquilizer. "Cat valium" is another one that reminds you that ketamine is best left to the vets. Speaking of rhymes, some street names come from a rhyme with the drug's real name. "Regretamine" has a lot of truth to it. "Green," on the other hand, does not—ketamine is colorless.

Don't be fooled into thinking K is super just because some people call it "Super K" or "Super acid." Really, just stay away from anything with a K—"Triple K," "K-Hole," "Keezy," "Kit-Kat," and "Kenny" are all other names for ketamine. And there are even more names being thought up all the time.

Green Super K

Kit-Kat

Special K

Ketamine

Vitamin K

with the ketamine. When you take illegal drugs at a club or elsewhere, you can never be sure just what you're getting.

The best way to avoid ketamine is the same as with any other drug: If someone offers you a strange powder, pill, or other substance at a bar, club, or party, just don't take it. Be especially careful not to accept drinks, even from friends, unless you saw the drink being made and it was given directly to you. You can't smell or taste ketamine, so it is sometimes used to drug people without their knowledge. Ketamine can knock you out and make you forget what happened to you. This makes it a very dangerous drug sometimes used to assault or even rape drugged victims.

Chapter 4

CRYSTAL METH
Shattered Lives

One of the most dangerous and damaging drugs is meth-amphetamine, also known as crystal meth. The terrible effects of meth addiction are so horrifying that one might wonder how someone could ever become addicted to it. The scary truth is that it's very easy, as a young woman named Carren Clem learned.

Carren didn't seem like the kind of kid who would use drugs. She had a happy childhood filled with violin lessons and horseback riding. Her father was a police officer who dealt with drugs and made sure his children knew how bad they were. However, when Carren moved to a new school, she began to have social problems. She often felt as though she didn't fit in. Unfortunately, this led her to befriend the wrong person.

A documentary film, *Saving Carren*, tells Carren Clem's story of addiction and recovery.

Carren's new "friend" lured her to a drug dealer's house, where she was given alcohol with date rape drugs and then was sexually assaulted. Unfortunately, like many victims of sexual assault, Carren felt confused and ashamed. The resulting depression drove her to more drinking and drugs—often bought from the very dealer who had raped her. After being sexually assaulted by a group of people at a party, again after having drugs slipped into her drink, she chose to go to a new school.

Carren had even more problems at the new school because she was still haunted by what had happened to her. She eventually left school to work as a telemarketer, an often stressful job that involves trying to sell things to people over the phone. This was when she really began to party. It wasn't long before someone offered her a "pick-me-up"—what she didn't know was that this "pick-me-up" was crystal meth. You might think that just trying meth once couldn't be that bad, but for Carren once was enough. The high from the meth was so strong that she couldn't deal with coming down, and she was hooked immediately. It took only a week for her to become a serious addict, using meth several times a day.

The life of a meth addict is not fun. Carren's parents gave her a choice: She could give up drugs, or she could leave their home with only the clothes on her back. Carren chose to leave. Without support, she turned to theft and sleeping around to get drugs. She was desperate and miserable. She was so miserable, in fact, that she tried to kill herself. Some of the people she thought were her friends gave her huge

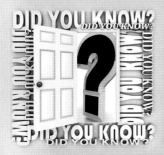

Amphetamine

One amphetamine that often leads to abuse is called . . . amphetamine. A little confusing? It's actually pretty simple— amphetamine is a lot like crystal meth, but not as intense. Like crystal meth, amphetamine can give a brief sense of intense pleasure (called euphoria). Unfortunately, this euphoria comes at a steep price. Dangerous side effects (such as increased heart rate and blood pressure) become even more common as people become habitual users. Over time, users also develop tolerance to the feelings of pleasure—that is, it takes more and more of the drug to get the same effect. Higher doses of the drug lead to even more severe side effects.

Amphetamine was first created in the 1930s, where it was used to help people stay awake, lose weight, or concentrate more easily. By the 1960s, however, widespread abuse of the drug led to it becoming very strictly controlled. Amphetamine is still sometimes prescribed as a medicine, usually to help combat behavioral disorders in children (though it's generally prescribed in very low doses.) However, just like meth, amphetamine is easy to become addicted to and easy to abuse. Never, ever take medicines that haven't been prescribed by your doctor, or take medicines in doses different than what's explained to you by your doctor or pharmacist.

amounts of drugs and alcohol. She took them, but instead of killing her, the drugs made her dreadfully, painfully sick.

It was then that Carren realized she needed to change her life.

Carren was lucky. She hit bottom before her meth use killed her, and now she is in recovery. She only used meth for six months, but her treatment took about 18 months, and her recovery is a lifetime ordeal. Today, she has a job, a husband, and a family, and she works to help keep other kids from making the mistakes she made. But even so, methamphetamine has left her damaged.

Meth use can damage the brain, and to this day Carren has problems with stress. She even continues to get powerful cravings for the highly addictive drug. If Carren hadn't been shocked into changing her life, crystal meth could have killed her—just like it kills thousands of people every year.[1,2]

Metham-what?

Methamphetamine is a pretty big word. What you should know is that "crystal meth" is a kind of amphetamine—a group of drugs that are stimulants, or "uppers." These drugs make people feel more excited and alert, and might cause other effects, like hallucinations. There are a lot of amphetamines with a lot of different effects. One, ephedrine, is a drug that has been used in medicine for thousands of years, although it is now known to have some dangerous side effects. Another is ecstasy, which you read about in Chapter Two.

Some people use over-the-counter cold medicines to make crystal meth.

Crystal meth is a powerful amphetamine. Like other drugs, it is sometimes used medically, but today that's very rare. Most often, meth is made illegally and sold on the street. Making meth is a major operation—it can get you killed even faster than becoming an addict.[3]

Making meth is often called "cooking," and just like real cooking there are recipes. A lot of those recipes use over-the-counter cold medicine. These medicines contain a drug called pseudoephedrine—a relatively safe kind of amphetamine. Because these medicines are so popular for making meth, many pharmacies now keep close track of who buys them.

Cold medicine may not sound too scary, but some of the other ingredients for making meth are much worse. There are volatile (highly unstable) chemicals, including acids and solvents (chemicals that dissolve other substances). Even worse, all these things react with each other. Chemical reactions can be very powerful. You've probably seen what happens when baking soda mixes with vinegar. That's nothing compared to what can happen when cooking meth goes wrong! Deadly fires can start seemingly out of nowhere. Poisonous gases can be released, asphyxiating you before you even realize you made a mistake. And sometimes the whole thing just explodes like a bomb!

Methamphetamine gets the name "crystal meth" because when all the chemistry is done, the drug settles into flat, glassy crystals. These crystals are usually ground into powder and snorted or smoked. Unfortunately, meth is often cooked badly and ends up tainted with chemicals

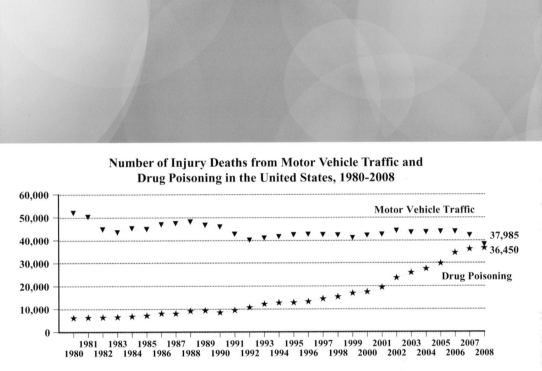

Number of Injury Deaths from Motor Vehicle Traffic and Drug Poisoning in the United States, 1980-2008

Source: Center for Substance Abuse Research, University of Maryland, College Park

By 2008, drug poisoining deaths approached the same number as deaths due to motor vehicle traffic.

even more poisonous than meth alone. Drug dealers don't make the most reliable chemists!

The danger isn't the only reason not to deal meth. Being caught with large quantities of meth can get you a long prison term—even a life sentence. Possession alone can get you up to five years in prison.

A High That Kills

Few other drugs have side effects as dangerous, unpleasant, and downright disgusting as crystal meth. People take meth because for a little while it makes them feel good. Like many other amphetamines, it makes them feel more alert and energetic. It even makes them feel happy while they're still high. But these feelings are nothing compared to the way crystal meth wrecks your mind and your body.

Meth messes your body up so badly that it doesn't know what to do with itself. It can make your heart beat dangerously fast, slow it to a crawl, or make it skip. It can give you dry skin or acne. It can cause diarrhea or constipation (the inability to move your bowels). It can give you high blood pressure or low blood pressure. It can make you shake, make you feel unbearably hot, blur your vision, or make your body go numb. It can even make you anorexic—that is, you don't want to eat enough to survive, so you slowly starve. And that's just the start.

Meth doesn't just make you feel more alert—it can send your brain into overdrive. It makes people angrier and more aggressive, sometimes to the point of violence. It also creates compulsive, destructive behaviors. People on meth sometimes compulsively pick at their skin, leaving ugly scars. They often grind their teeth. They have hallucinations and become paranoid, feeling that everyone is against them. Meth can make you feel indestructible, even while you're destroying yourself.

If you think that's bad, here's the thing—all of these things can happen to you just from using meth once. The long-term effects of meth use take all these terrible side effects to the extreme. A tell-tale sign of meth addiction is a condition called "meth mouth." Because of tooth-grinding, dry-mouth, and a tendency to forget to brush and floss, meth users lose teeth very quickly. Worse, while meth's effects on your heart and blood pressure are always dangerous, over time it becomes more and more likely that you'll have a sudden heart attack, very possibly killing you. You may also have a stroke, which can kill you or leave you permanently disabled. Meth's effects on your brain and nervous system can lead to convulsions—uncontrollable shaking and spasms. It can also lead from paranoia and aggression into suicidal depression or violent insanity. Meth not only hurts you, but it can lead you to hurt yourself and others.[4]

When You Can't Stop

Methamphetamine is very, very addictive. Although all drugs can be psychologically addictive, meth is also physically addictive. You don't just like meth, meth convinces your body that you need meth. It's very difficult to break free of an addiction when both your mind and your body are telling you that you need to keep using the drug that's tormenting you.

Talk to a trusted adult if you have concerns about drug use.

The unpleasant symptoms of meth withdrawal don't make it any easier. Luckily, quitting meth isn't usually dangerous for your body, but it doesn't feel too good, either. Addicts trying to quit feel tired and "used up," like they don't have the energy to do anything. Unsurprisingly, they often feel depressed, and nothing seems to make them feel good. They may be irritable, restless, and generally unpleasant to be around. All this makes it tough for addicts to stay clean.

Just like with Carren, sometimes meth does damage that never goes away completely. Even addicts who successfully kick their habit and clean up their lives often have to live with scars, missing teeth, or general ill-health from months or years of abuse. They may suffer from mood swings, depression, and even "flashbacks" where their drug-fueled aggression and anger come back for no reason. While recovery is possible, there's no substitute for never abusing meth in the first place. If you or a friend has tried methamphetamine, talk to a trustworthy adult right away.

The Price We All Pay

Methamphetamine isn't just a problem for the people who use it—meth makes the world worse for all of us. Thousands die from meth use every year, and they leave behind friends and family who suffer without them. Meth is also strongly associated with violent crime. It's not hard to see why— meth addicts are more likely to be impulsive and violent. People suffering from powerful addictions will often steal or even kill to get the drugs they need.

THE NAME
Game

Like most drugs, methamphetamine goes by many names. You already know "meth" and "crystal meth." Sometimes it's just called "crystal," or a similar name like "rock," "glass," or "shard." Other times it's compared to ice, leading to names like "cold" and, well, "ice." Some other names you may have heard are "speed," "crank," and "tina"—all of these usually refer to meth or similar drugs.

Because meth is so addictive, it is well-known around the world. Some names that come from foreign languages include "shabu," "batu," "scanté," "piko," "ya ba," "bato," and "tik."

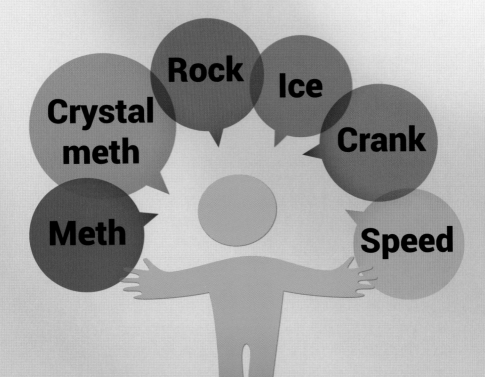

Many meth users end up unemployed and homeless, while others irresponsibly spread diseases they pick up due to their lack of self-control. Meth labs can even start dangerous fires. Between meth users hurting themselves and hurting other people, meth is involved in as many as 8 percent of all emergency room visits in the United States!

Crime, disease, and death are the price society pays because people become methamphetamine addicts.

Chapter 5

GHB AND ROHYPNOL
"Date Rape" Drugs

Samantha Reid told her mother she was going out to see a movie with some friends. But she was bending the truth a bit. Fifteen-year-old Samantha and her friends Melanie, fourteen, and Jessica, fifteen, had decided to go out and have fun with some older boys. They eventually ended up at the apartment of a twenty-five-year-old friend of the boys, where some of them drank alcohol and used marijuana. Samantha had a Mountain Dew. She said to Melanie that the drink "tasted funny," but decided to finish it anyway. If she hadn't, she might be alive today.

Samantha was unaware that the girls' drinks had been spiked with a drug called gamma-Hydroxybutyric acid, popularly known as GHB. The boys later said they had added the drug to the drinks in order to make the party

Be aware and be smart. Drinks at a party could be spiked with GHB or other drugs.

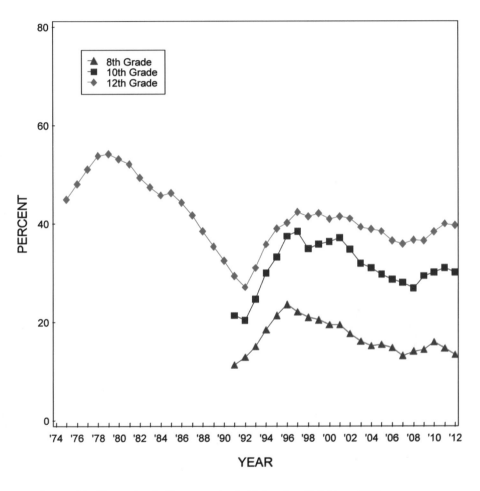

Any Illicit Drug: **Trends in Annual Use**
Grades 8, 10, and 12

Legend:
- ▲ 8th Grade
- ■ 10th Grade
- ◆ 12th Grade

Y-axis: PERCENT (0 to 80)
X-axis: YEAR ('74 to '12)

Source: The Monitoring the Future study, the University of Michigan, 2012.

Illicit drug use by students in grades eight, ten, and twelve each year from 1974 to 2012

more "lively." It quickly became the opposite. Samantha fell asleep on the sofa soon after finishing her drink. When she started throwing up, the boys brought her into the bathroom and laid her down on the floor. Melanie also passed out and was laid down next to her. Jessica didn't touch the drink she'd been given, and didn't become sick. The boys dawdled before taking the girls to get medical help. By the time they arrived at the hospital, Samantha had died. Melanie remained in a coma, unable to wake up, for several hours. The boys had lied about where they had been and what they had been doing. But when Melanie woke up, she told the truth to the police. Justice was eventually done, but Samantha had paid the price.[1]

GHB?

Gamma-Hydroxybutyric acid is usually in the form of an odorless, colorless liquid. It looks just like water. It can also be made into a white powder or a pill. In any form, you can't see it or smell it once it's been added to something. It barely has any taste, so it can be hard to detect when it's placed in a drink—especially one with a strong taste, such as an alcoholic beverage. GHB first became popular in the 1980s when people thought it was a safe and natural health supplement. It was said to have many different uses. People thought it could be used as an antidepressant, and could help you sleep. It was also popular with bodybuilders, who thought it helped build muscle. But soon people started overdosing on GHB, and officials began to realize that it was dangerous.

Rohypnol

Unfortunately, GHB is very easy to make. Most GHB is made by people in their homes. It can be made in a person's kitchen. It's also very easy to make wrong, which takes this drug from dangerous to deadly. Some people make it with dangerous chemicals such as drain cleaner or paint remover. These can cause chemical burns on the throat when the drug is swallowed.

Heather's Story: Rohypnol

Heather MacPhee didn't keep track of her drink when she went out one night, and a little white pill was slipped into it without her knowledge. She started to feel funny, like she was really drunk. She couldn't walk or talk properly. Luckily, her friends noticed she was acting strangely. She woke up in the hospital the next morning unable to remember anything that had happened the night before.[2]

The drug Heather was slipped was called Rohypnol. Like with Samantha Reid, someone had probably hoped to make Heather more "lively." Instead, she almost lost her life. Rohypnol is another drug that is very difficult to detect. It has no smell, color, or taste, so it's impossible to know if someone might have put it into your drink.

Rohypnol is a brand name of the drug flunitrazepam. It was originally developed in 1975 as a sedative, which is a medication to help people sleep. It relaxes the muscles and makes you calm and tired. It is used legally in many countries to help people with sleeping and anxiety disorders, but it's illegal in the United States. Most Rohypnol in the United States has been smuggled in from Europe or Mexico.[3]

Since Rohypnol is a drug brand made by a specific company, it is mostly made in labs. After it started to be misused, the company that manufactures it made it slower to dissolve. They also added a blue color to it. But fake Rohypnol is also made illegally by amateur chemists. This can be even more dangerous than the real stuff.

"Date Rape" Drugs

You may have heard of drugs like GHB and Rohypnol being called "date rape" drugs. Because these drugs make people sleepy and forgetful, they are sometimes used for sexual assault. A person will secretly slip a drug such as GHB or Rohypnol into someone else's drink and then wait until they fall asleep or are incoherent. Then they take advantage of the drugged person, either with sexual contact or sometimes just by robbing them. The person who was drugged often won't remember what happened to them or who they were with. The drugs are called "date rape" because they are often slipped to unsuspecting people by someone they went out to a club or party with. A lot of people think date rape is only a problem for women, but anyone can be drugged and taken advantage of.

Sexual assault is a serious crime, and slipping people drugs is a serious crime, too. If you are caught with GHB or Rohypnol you can spend several years in jail. If you commit a sexual assault with the aid of a drug, you can spend up to 15 years in jail.

Go to the hospital if you suspect that you or someone you know was given Rohypnol or another dangerous drug.

So How Do You Know?

How can you tell if you or a friend have been given a date rape drug without your knowledge? GHB and Rohypnol have similar effects. They start about fifteen minutes to half an hour after the drug has been taken and can last for hours—sometimes even days. People under the influence of GHB or Rohypnol will act like they're very drunk. This might make them seem more fun and talkative for a while, even if they're usually very shy. But these effects will soon end. Their speech will become slurred and less intelligible. They will start to feel very weak. They may become very sleepy and even pass out. Other possible symptoms include nausea, vomiting, and numbness. In extreme cases a person who has been drugged may experience heightened anxiety or hallucinations. These drugs may cause problems with breathing, so it's important to get help immediately if you or a friend has any of these symptoms and you suspect a drug may be involved.

Sometimes drinks that have been dosed will have foam or a ring of residue on them, but sometimes they won't. If you start to feel drunk or otherwise not yourself after having a nonalcoholic drink, you may have been given a drug without your knowledge.

Staying Safe

While many people know that date rape drugs are involved in cases of sexual assault, most people don't realize that alcohol is much more dangerous. Many more sexual assaults happen to people who are simply drunk on alcohol. Alcohol

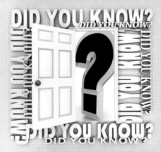

CRACKING
Down

At the time Samantha Reid died, kits for making GHB were legal in many states. This means they were also easy to get in states where GHB was illegal. People used the Internet to buy kits from states where the drug was legal. After Samantha's death—and the death of another teenaged girl, Hillory Farias—U.S. lawmakers started to take notice of this dangerous drug. In 2000, the United States Congress passed a bill to make GHB a Schedule I drug, which means it's one of the most dangerous drugs available. People caught making or selling GHB can spend five years to life in prison. The bill also banned some of the substances that could be used to make GHB and set up guidelines for the government to do more to inform the public about the drug. It was called, fittingly, the Hillory J. Farias and Samantha Reid Date-Rape Drug Prohibition Act of 2000.

While this bill is still in place, GHB was made legal in the United States in 2002 for very specific medical uses. It can help people who have narcolepsy, a disorder that causes a person to fall asleep at unpredictable times. The use of GHB in this manner is very tightly controlled.[5]

makes you lose your inhibitions, which means you don't think twice about doing things that might not be good for you. People who use alcohol also have a harder time fighting back if they are approached in a way they don't like. Even without being drugged, a significant amount of alcohol can make you pass out and forget what happened. The best way to protect yourself from becoming a victim at a party is to not get drunk. But you should always take precautious with your drinks when you go out, just to be safe.

Scientists have been developing sensors that help detect date rape drugs in drinks. In some places you may be able to buy coasters or strips that will detect drugs in drinks. But these technologies may not always be accessible, and there are only certain drugs they can detect.[4] The best way to protect yourself from drugs such as GHB and Rohypnol is to always keep track of your drink. Whether you're out on the town or just at a party with friends, keep an eye on your cup. If you lose sight of your drink or have to put it down for a few minutes to go to the bathroom, empty it and get a new one. Don't let someone you don't know or don't trust offer to get you a drink—ask if you can get it yourself, or if you can have an unopened can or bottle.

If you or a friend starts to feel sick and you suspect you may have been drugged, it's important to get to a safe place and call 911. Have a friend you trust go with you in case you start feeling woozy or lose consciousness. If a friend passes out, make sure you lie them on their side in case they vomit. A person who vomits while lying on his back may choke.

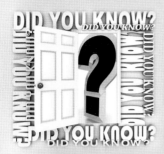

THE NAME
Game

Date rape drugs go by many different names on the street. Tell a trustworthy adult if you hear any of these terms and suspect someone is talking about illegal drugs.

For GHB:
energy drink
gamma 10
G-juice
goop
liquid ecstasy
liquid G

For Rohypnol/Flunitrazepam:
forget-me pill
la rocha
R-2
rib
Roche
roofies
rope

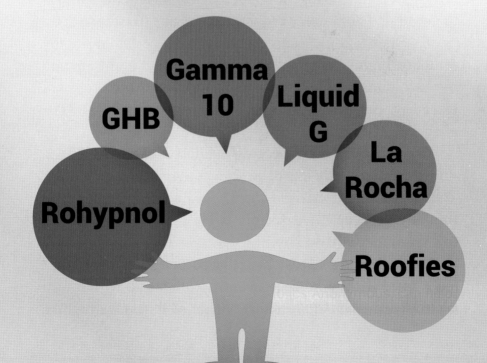

If you can, bring the glass or cup that held the contaminated drink with you to the police station or hospital so it can be tested for drug residue.

When you get to the hospital, make sure they take a urine sample to test for traces of drugs. If you wake up after falling unconscious and suspect you may have been sexually assaulted, don't take a shower, use the bathroom, or change your clothes. You may feel like you want to get clean, but there could be important evidence about what happened to you on your clothes or in your body. To get checked out, go immediately to a hospital or police station.

Assault Aside

Although drugs like Rohypnol and GHB are best known now as date rape drugs, some people take them on purpose to get high. People may tell you that drugs like these are a "safe," "natural," or "hangover free" way of feeling really drunk or high. They may even tell you GHB will help you increase muscle or get better at sports. But these drugs are extremely easy to overdose on if you're not careful, and the effects can be fatal.

Some people even become addicted to these drugs. Rohypnol especially has been shown to cause dependence. That is to say, it tricks people's brains and bodies into thinking they can't live without it. People who are addicted to a substance will do anything to make sure they can have it. They may lie or steal in order to get their next "fix." Many people stay addicted to drugs because withdrawal symptoms are too unpleasant. Withdrawal from a drug like

Rohypnol can cause soreness, headaches, hallucinations, and sometimes even seizures. It is very important to get help if you or a friend are addicted to one of these drugs. Talk to a trustworthy adult if you or a friend is in need of help overcoming an addiction.

Chapter 6

LSD
A Bad Trip

Seventeen-year-old Timothy Castaneda, like many teens, went out to have fun with his friends on a Friday night. They decided to have a party in the woods behind a local movie theater. As the night went on, Timothy decided it would be fun to have some drugs at the party. He called a friend to bring a drug called LSD, a powerful hallucinogen. A hallucinogen is a drug that alters your state of mind. It makes you hallucinate, so you see and hear things that aren't really there. Some people think this kind of experience is fun. Unfortunately for Timothy, his experience was anything but fun.

Timothy took two "hits," or doses, of LSD. According to his friends, he soon started "freaking out." This lasted for several hours, until Timothy finally collapsed and started having seizures. He started foaming and bleeding from the mouth. Eventually he stopped breathing. His friends called for an ambulance, which rushed Timothy to a hospital. By the time he got there, he had already suffered extensive brain damage. He died a week later.[1]

Lysergic-who?

LSD is short for lysergic acid diethylamide. This drug is also commonly known as acid. It was first developed in Switzerland in 1938 by chemist Albert Hofmann. He was trying to make a drug that could help stimulate bloodflow and breathing, but LSD didn't give the results he wanted. He didn't find out the actual effects of LSD until several years later, by accident. After that the company he had been working for decided to make and market LSD. In the 1940s, 50s, and 60s, this drug was used in experiments by psychologists because its effects are similar to certain types of psychosis. LSD became especially popular in the 1960s among the "hippie" counterculture, who used it as an escape from normal society. The drug was even used by the United States government in experiments for possible military uses. Officials thought a drug like LSD, which can cause extreme hallucinations, might help in making enemies confused and afraid.[2]

However, LSD was not destined for any of these uses. It was banned by the U.S. government in 1965. Since then it has had periods of popularity as an illegal drug at clubs and parties, especially in the late 1990s and early 2000s. It is now a Schedule I illegal drug, which means it is considered to be one of the most dangerous drugs. The first time a

A party in the woods turned out to be Timothy Castaneda's last party.

person is caught with LSD he can spend up to a year in prison or pay a $1,000 fine. There are higher penalties for being caught more than once, and even higher penalties for making or selling the drug.

LSD is a synthetic drug, which means it's made in laboratories. Since LSD is now an illegal drug, these laboratories are illegal operations. The chemicals used to make it can be very dangerous and are very difficult to get. The main ingredient, though, is a type of fungus that grows on rye and other grain plants!

A Drug of All Shapes and Sizes

LSD is odorless, colorless, and mosty tasteless. It can be made in many different forms, including pills (also called "microdots"), squares of gelatin ("windowpanes"), and liquid. It most commonly comes on sheets of paper (sometimes called "loony toons"). LSD in crystal form is dissolved and paper is dipped into the solution. Then the paper is dried and perforated (poked with holes for easy cutting or tearing) into tiny squares that are licked or chewed and swallowed. The paper will often be printed with designs to make it look cute or attractive, but looks can be deceiving. One "hit," or dose, of LSD is one square. A single sheet of paper can contain up to 900 hits. This drug is very powerful, and a person can feel the effects from even a very tiny amount—about the same weight as two grains of salt.[3]

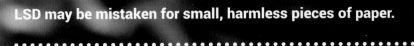

LSD may be mistaken for small, harmless pieces of paper.

Tripping

The effects of LSD are often known as "tripping." LSD alters people's perceptions so they perceive things around them differently. Hallucinogens like LSD "scramble" perceptions. For example, someone might taste a sound. The experience starts about an hour after the drug is taken and can last for twelve hours or more afterward.

The primary effects of LSD are on the visual part of the brain. People who have taken LSD see colors brighter. They may see patterns or halos of light on objects. Things that are stationary may appear to move on their own. Taking LSD can also cause auditory (hearing) or sensory hallucinations. You may hear things that aren't real or feel like something is happening to you when it isn't, like someone touching you or bugs crawling on your skin.

LSD users will often lose their sense of self or time, and forget who or where they are. They might not recognize friends or family and become suspicious of them, or even attack them. People having a "bad trip" may become extremely frightened or intensely depressed. They may experience heightened anxiety or panic attacks. They may become extremely paranoid or even terrified, and may even get dizzy or nauseous. It's impossible to tell when taking LSD if you'll have a good trip or a bad trip, even if you've taken it before. Some people experience what are known as "flashbacks." They randomly return to LSD hallucinations without warning, sometimes weeks or months after having taken the drug. There is no known way to stop these flashbacks from happening, and no way to tell how many a person might have, even after a single dose of LSD.

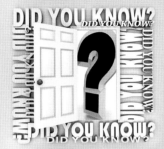

LSD FOR
Good?

As you read, LSD was originally discovered because a chemist was attempting to make a new drug for medical use. He only found out the effects of LSD after making a batch and accidentally getting some on his fingers, which he touched his mouth with or otherwise ingested. After the effects were known, people started trying to think of ways in which LSD and its hallucinogenic effects could be used for medicine.

The drug was embraced by psychologists, who used it to treat people with mental disorders. They thought that by producing hallucinations they could get patients to open up to them or to experience "spiritual awakenings" that would help make them better. They also tried to use the drug to scare alcoholics into quitting their alcohol addiction.

Doctors tried LSD for various uses for decades, but it was never proven to be helpful in treating any disorder. In the 1970s the National Institute for Mental Health officially stated that LSD wasn't useful in treating mental health. However, in the early 2000s, researchers started tests to see if LSD could be used to help senior citizens as they deal with stress and health issues at the end of their lives. They also started trying again to use it to help people with alcohol addiction.[5]

THE NAME Game

LSD goes by many names on the street, the most popular of which is "acid." Listed below are some other names people use for this drug. Tell a trustworthy adult if you hear someone using any of these terms and suspect they are talking about illegal drugs: blotter, California sunshine, Cid, dots, electric Kool-Aid, tab, zen.

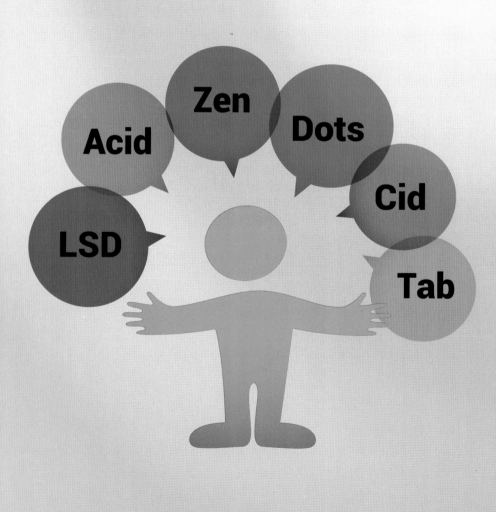

The physical effects of LSD are usually mild. They can include changes in blood pressure and body temperature, which can be dangerous if not taken care of. Other effects can include dizziness, dilated pupils, and tingling of hands and feet. The real danger from LSD isn't usually from what happens to your body, though; it's from what happens to your mind. People who are experiencing hallucinations on LSD are often unaware of what's really going on around them. They may get themselves into situations that are dangerous, like walking out into traffic or falling down stairs or out of windows.

As with any drug, the biggest danger can be in thinking you know what you're getting into. Since illegal drugs operate outside of drug regulations, there's no way to know if you're buying what you think you're buying. If a dealer or chemist gets the chemicals wrong or intentionally adds something dangerous into the mix, you won't know until it's too late. In 2012, Australian teenager Nick Mitchell and his friend bought what they thought was regular LSD, but ended up with a batch that proved fatal for Nick. He suffered from breathing problems and died after taking the drug. His friend had intense hallucinations and was hit by a car while running naked into the street.[4]

When You Can't Stop

LSD is addictive, though people are slower to become addicted than with some other drugs. People who enjoy its effects sometimes keep coming back for more. They spend too much time in a dream world, hallucinating their life away, when they have other obligations. They may forget to eat or take care of their personal hygiene. These dangers can add to the dangers of not being fully aware of their surroundings. And after multiple "trips" a user may find the effects of LSD aren't as fun, and turn to other, more dangerous drugs to get high. If you or a friend is losing track of real life because of repeated LSD use, talk to a trustworthy adult. It's important to get help before turning to drugs that can put your life in immediate danger.

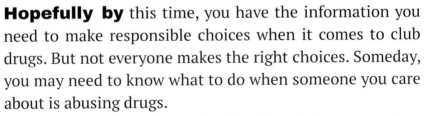

Chapter 7

GETTING *Help*

Hopefully by this time, you have the information you need to make responsible choices when it comes to club drugs. But not everyone makes the right choices. Someday, you may need to know what to do when someone you care about is abusing drugs.

It can be tough to confront a friend about a serious issue—no one likes to feel like they're butting in where they're not wanted. The thing is, if you ignore the problem, it's likely everyone else will, too. Remember, nobody gets into drugs because they want to become an addict. If a friend has a problem, he may not even realize it until someone confronts him about it.

There are some important things you should remember when making the decision to confront a friend about his

Being a good listener or confiding in a supportive friend are important steps when dealing with drug abuse.

drug use. First, wait until he's sober to do it. You want to make sure he's capable of making a good decision when you talk to him. Second, talk in private. It can be hard for people to admit mistakes in front of others. Talking to them about drugs in front of others can embarrass them and make them angry. Third, be prepared: It'll be a lot easier to say your piece if you know what you want to say ahead of time.

There are a lot of ways to be prepared. You should think of specific times that your friend's behavior made you worried or upset and be ready to talk about them. It might also be helpful to be ready to talk about the consequences of what can happen when someone abuses drugs—the health problems, the legal consequences, and the other risks they're taking. And you should think about some suggestions for what your friend can do. Just telling him he has a problem without offering any solutions usually isn't so helpful.

It's important to listen to your friend and respond to what he says. Remember, you can't force him to take your advice. But if he knows that you're listening to his side of things he may be more likely to listen to yours, too.

It's not fun to think about, but there may be a time when you have to go to an adult for help. Obviously, no one wants to feel like they're tattling or getting a friend in trouble. But if you think a friend's drug use is becoming a threat to his own safety, or the safety of others, you shouldn't stand by and let someone get hurt. There's a difference between going to a parent or counselor because you want to get someone in trouble and going to a parent or counselor because you want to get someone out of trouble.

Go out with friends and get involved in activities that do not involve drugs.

· ·

Treatment for Drug Addiction

But what if it's you who has the problem? Obviously, the best way to avoid addiction is to avoid drugs in the first place. But if you make a mistake and realize that you're developing a problem, there are ways to get help.

The first thing to remember is that you probably will need help. It's tempting to think you can break your self-destructive habits alone, but this is rarely true. Needing help from your friends, your family, and even professional counselors or therapists isn't a sign of weakness—it's a sign you're taking your recovery seriously.

Make your friends and family part of your recovery. Tell your friends that you're not going to be using drugs anymore, and ask them to hold you to that. Tell your family that you're going to need their support sometimes. If you need someone to talk to, or just to be around people who'll help you think about something other than your problem, figure out who those people are and ask them to be there for you.

Try to avoid places where drugs and alcohol are available. Turning down a party or a night out at a club may not be fun, but it can help. The best way to avoid falling back into bad habits is to avoid the situations that lead to those habits. Go out with friends or family that don't use drugs, or do things where drugs are unlikely to come up, like movies, sports, or games.

If these steps don't seem to be enough, don't despair. Talk to your parents, a teacher, or a school counselor you trust about getting help from professionals. There are lots of ways to try to beat your problems. It'll be work—maybe

DRUG
Schedules?

The United States Drug Enforcement Agency (DEA) is a law enforcement agency that fights drug smuggling and dealing—a kind of national police department that just deals with drugs. The DEA classifies drugs according to different "schedules" of "controlled substances"—drugs and other chemicals that are often illegal to own or trade. The schedules are as follows:

Schedule I: Highly addictive drugs that have no recognized medical use. These drugs are considered very dangerous.

Schedule II: Drugs that are very addictive, but generally less dangerous than Schedule I drugs. They may be occasionally prescribed medically.

Schedule III: Drugs that are less addictive than Schedule I or II drugs, but are still at significant risk of abuse. Many of them are relatively common medicines.

Schedule IV: Drugs that have low addictive potential and aren't at high risk of abuse. Many of these are common medicines.

Schedule V: Drugs that are at very low risk for abuse. These are generally used for minor medical issues, like mild pain relief or helping upset stomachs.

The penalties for possessing or dealing drugs vary widely by which schedule of drug they are. Most of the drugs mentioned in this book are Schedule I or II drugs— the most dangerous kinds.[2]

PLACES TO GO
For Help

If you need help, the best place to find it is from an adult you trust—like a parent or other relative, a teacher, or a guidance counselor. But if you don't have an adult that you feel you can confide in, there are other places you can turn to for help. A few of them include:

Narcotics Anonymous: Narcotics Anonymous is an organization where people can find support for kicking a habit with drugs without having to give their full names. Despite the name, Narcotics Anonymous is there to help people with any drug or alcohol addiction. Go to www.na.org to find a meeting near you.

The National Alcoholism and Substance Abuse Information Center (NASAIC): The NASAIC runs a database of local drug and alcohol treatment options around the country. You can go to www.addictioncareoptions.com to search their site for organizations near you that can help. Or, you can chat with one of their staff members to help you find a treatment program or rehab center.

The Substance Abuse and Mental Health Services Administration (SAMHSA): SAMHSA is a branch of the U.S. government that provides services to people with substance abuse problems or mental health issues. Go to www.samhsa
.gov for information about the services they offer as well as to use their treatment locator to find help in your area.

Trained professionals at rehab and support groups can help recovering drug users get healthy and drug-free.

EMERGENCY ROOM *VISITS*

The Drug Abuse Warning Network (DAWN) estimates that in 2011 there were about 280,000 drug-related ER visits by adolescents aged 12 to 17, of which 181,005 visits involved the use of illicit drugs, alcohol, or intentional misuse or abuse of pharmaceuticals (e.g., prescription medicines, over-the-counter remedies, and dietary supplements). On a typical day in 2011, there were 777 drug-related ER visits for adolescents aged 12 to 17, of which 496 involved the use of illegal drugs or the misuse or abuse of pharmaceuticals. On a typical day in 2011, the listed substances were involved at the following levels:

- 110 involved alcohol only;
- 87 involved alcohol in combination with other drugs;
- 165 involved marijuana;
- 20 involved MDMA (i.e., Ecstasy), LSD, PCP, or other hallucinogens;
- 16 involved cocaine;
- 16 involved illicit amphetamines or methamphetamine;
- 7 involved inhalants;
- 6 involved heroin;
- 74 involved prescription or nonprescription pain relievers, 26 of which involved narcotic pain relievers (e.g., hydrocodone, oxycodone);
- 32 involved antidepressants or antipsychotics;
- 31 involved benzodiazepines; and
- 11 involved attention-deficit/hyperactivity disorder (ADHD) medications.

Source: 2011 SAMHSA Drug Abuse Warning Network (DAWN)

the hardest work you've ever done—but it's possible as long as you don't give up.[1]

There are a lot of ways to have fun out there in the world, but remember that there are always risks. The dangers of drugs—even drugs "everyone" is doing—are severe. When you have to decide whether or not to do drugs, think about those risks and maybe think of another way to have fun. Nobody is so bored that they need to do something stupid to have a good time.

Chapter Notes

Chapter 1 — Danger in the Club

1. "Dealing with Peer Pressure," *KidsHealth*, <http://kidshealth.org/kid/feeling/friend/peer_pressure.html> (February 21, 2013).
2. "Fact Sheets: Binge Drinking," The Centers for Disease Control and Prevention, November 7, 2012, <http://www.guardian.co.uk/society/2012/feb/02/deputy-head-drug-culture-son-death-ecstasy> (February 21, 2013).

Chapter 2 — MDMA/ECSTASY: A Night Out Turns Deadly

1. Richard Saville, "Father condemns 'hedonistic drug culture' after talented teenage son's ecstasy death," *The Telegraph*, June 3, 2011, <http://www.telegraph.co.uk/news/uknews/8555108/Father-condemns-hedonistic-drug-culture-after-talented-teenage-sons-ecstasy-death.html> (January 9, 2013).
2. Steve Morris, "Deputy head criticises UK drugs culture after son's death from ecstasy," *The Guardian*, February 2, 2012, <http://www.guardian.co.uk/society/2012/feb/02/deputy-head-drug-culture-son-death-ecstasy> (January 9, 2013).
3. Matthew Holehouse, "Father attacks celebrities who 'glorify' drug taking," *The Telegraph*, February 3, 2012, <http://www.telegraph.co.uk/news/uknews/law-and-order/9058266/Father-attacks-celebrities-who-glorify-drug-taking.html> (January 9, 2013).
4. John Philip Jenkins, "Ecstasy," *Britannica Online Encyclopedia*, n.d., <http://www.britannica.com/EBchecked/topic/378657/Ecstasy> (January 27, 2013).

5. Gerry J. Gilmore, "DoD Attacks Ecstasy Drug Use," U.S. Department of Defense, September 7, 2000, <http://www.defense.gov/News/NewsArticle.aspx?ID=45469> (January 27, 2013).

6. "Research Report Series: MDMA (Ecstasy) Abuse," The Endowment for Human Development, April 2004, <http://www.ehd.org/health_ecstasy_7.php> (January 27, 2013).

7. National Institute on Drug Abuse, "Drug Facts: MDMA (Ecstasy)," n.d., <http://www.drugabuse.gov/publications/drugfacts/mdma-ecstasy> (February 5, 2013).

Chapter 3 — KETAMINE Bad Medicine

1. Lisa O'Kelly, "Every parent's worst nightmare: how ketamine killed our daughter," *The Guardian*, April 16, 2011, <http://www.guardian.co.uk/society/2011/apr/17/louise-cattell-parents-ketamine-campaign> (February 21, 2013).

2. Chris Greenwood, "Young fashion worker died in the bath after snorting horse tranquiliser drug Ketamine," *The Daily Mail*, May 27, 2011, <http://www.dailymail.co.uk/news/article-1391181/Louise-Cattell-fashion-worker-died-bath-snorting-Ketamine.html> (February 21, 2013).

3. Jo MacFarlane, "Hospitals battle with epidemic of party drug 'Special K' victims suffering with weak bladders," *The Daily Mail*, October 3, 2010, <http://www.dailymail.co.uk/news/article-1317191/Hospitals-battle-party-drug-Special-K-victims-weak-bladders.html> (February 21, 2013).

4. K. L. Jansen, "Non-medical use of ketamine," *US National Library of Medicine*, March 6, 1993, <http://www.ncbi.nlm.nih.gov/pmc/articles/PMC1676978/?tool=pmcentrez> (February 21, 2013).

Chapter 4
CRYSTAL METH
Shattered Lives

1. Carren Clem, "Conquering Meth Addiction: Carren Clem's Story," *WebMD*, May 28, 2010, <http://women.webmd.com/features/conquering-meth-addiction-carren-clems-story> (February 21, 2013).
2. Andrea Garrison, "Loss of Innocence with Ron and Carren Clem," *The Daily Mail*, October 30, 2008, <http://www.blogtalkradio.com/onlinewithandrea/2008/10/30/loss-of-innocence-with-ron-and-carren-clem> (February 21, 2013).
3. The Center for Substance Abuse Research, "Amphetamines," <http://www.cesar.umd.edu/cesar/drugs/amphetamines.asp> (February 21, 2013).
4. National Institute on Drug Abuse, "DrugFacts: Methamphetamine," March 2010, <http://www.drugabuse.gov/publications/drugfacts/methamphetamine> (February 21, 2013).

Chapter 5
ROHYPNOL AND GHB
"Date Rape" Drugs

1. Keith Bradsher, "3 Guilty of Manslaughter in Slipping Drug to Girl," *The New York Times*, March 15, 2000, <http://www.nytimes.com/2000/03/15/us/3-guilty-of-manslaughter-in-slipping-drug-to-girl.html> (February 17, 2013).
2. Heather MacPhee, "Date rape drug: A personal story," *Ellensburg Daily Record*, April 22, 1997, < http://news.google.com/newspapers?%20nid=860&dat=19970422&id=UQkfAAAAIBAJ&sjid=9MoEAAAAIBAJ&pg=6326,4203706> (February 17, 2013).

3. "Rohypnol," *BBC Health*, May 2011, < http://www.bbc.co.uk/ health/physical_health/conditions/rohypnol.shtml> (February 18, 2013).

4. "New Line of Defense Against Sexual Assault: Researchers Develop Pocket-sized Sensor to Detect "Date Rape" Drugs," *ScienceDaily*, August 9, 2011, < http://www.sciencedaily.com/ releases/2011/08/110809111818.htm > (February 23, 2013).

5. "Date rape drugs fact sheet," *Womenshealth.gov*, December 5, 2008, <http://www.womenshealth.gov/publications/ our-publications/fact-sheet/date-rape-drugs.cfm> (February 23, 2013).

Chapter 6

LSD
A Bad Trip

1. Adam Owens, "Father: Experimenting with drugs cost Apex teen his life," *WRAL.com*, October 25, 2012, < http://www. wral.com/father-experimenting-with-drugs-cost-apex-teen-his-life/11703049/ > (February 24, 2013).

2. Foundation for a Drug-free World, "LSD: A Short History," n.d., <http://www.drugfreeworld.org/drugfacts/lsd/a-short-history. html> (February 24, 2013).

3. Shanna Freeman, "How LSD Works," *howstuffworks.com*, n.d., <http://science.howstuffworks.com/lsd.htm> (February 24, 2013).

4. Richard Noone, "Warning to students of pill danger after the LSD death of teenager Nick Mitchell," *Herald Sun*, December 7, 2010, <http://www.heraldsun.com.au/news/national/warning-to-students-of-pill-danger-after-the-lsd-death-of-teenager-nick-mitchell/story-fndo317g-1226531614617> (February 25, 2013).

5. John Philip Jenkins, "LSD (drug)," *Britannica Online Encyclopedia*, n.d., <http://www.britannica.com/EBchecked/topic/350174/LSD> (February 25, 2013).

Chapter 7 — GETTING Help

1. "Dealing with Addiction," *TeensHealth*, <http://kidshealth.org/teen/your_mind/problems/addictions.html#> (February 21, 2013).
2. United States Drug Enforcement Administration, "Drug Scheduling," <http://www.justice.gov/dea/druginfo/ds.shtml> (February 21, 2013).

Glossary

addiction—Being unable, mentally or physically or both, to stop doing something.

amphetamine—A mood-altering drug that is used both legally and illegally.

anesthesiologist—A doctor who administers anesthetics.

anesthetic—A type of drug that reduces pain by reducing feeling.

antidepressant—A type of drug used to help treat clinical depression, which is a persistent feeling of sadness.

binge drinking—Drinking to excess over a short period of time.

convulsions—Sudden and uncontrollable moving of the body.

dehydration—The loss of water and salts essential for the body.

depressant—A type of drug that reduces your body's functions.

dopamine—A neurotransmitter (brain chemical) that controls the brain's reward and pleasure centers as well as your ability to pay attention.

hallucination—Experiencing things that aren't actually happening, such as seeing, hearing, or feeling something that isn't real.

hyperthermia—A condition in which the body's temperature is well above normal.

incontinence—Not being able to control urine or defecation (peeing or pooping).

inhibitions—Feelings of restraint.

marijuana—A common street and recreational drug that comes from the hemp plant.

neurons—Brain cells that transmit messages to each other.

neurotransmitters—Chemicals in the brain that help transmit messages.

norepinephrine—A neurotransmitter (brain chemical) that controls the body's fight-or-flight response.

panic attack—An episode of extreme fear and panic that can be paralyzing or cause other unpleasant physical symptoms.

pseudoephedrine—A legal drug used to treat sinus problems that can be used to make methamphetamine.

psychotherapy—A type of treatment of a mental illness or disorder using mental techniques.

rave—A type of all-night party, popular in many parts of the world, where light shows, dancing, and illegal drugs are often the focus.

sedative—A type of drug that makes someone calm or even fall asleep.

seizure—An episode of sudden, uncontrollable shaking of the body.

serotonin—A neurotransmitter (brain chemical) that regulates things like emotion, sleep, and pain response.

sober—Not under the influence of a drug, especially alcohol.

solvent—A substance that dissolves into another substance.

stimulant—A type of drug that speeds your body's functions.

stroke—An attack caused by reduced bloodflow to the brain, which can cause impairment or unconsciousness.

synthetic—Man-made.

tranquilizer—A type of drug that reduces tension.

volatile—Unstable.

withdrawal—To stop taking a substance one is addicted to; it can often cause unpleasant side-effects.

Organizations

Alcoholics Anonymous
A.A. World Services, Inc.
P.O. Box 459
New York, NY 10163
(212) 870-3400
<http://www.aa.org>

Al-Anon/Alateen
Al-Anon Family Group Headquarters
1600 Corporate Landing Parkway
Virginia Beach, VA 23454
(757) 563-1600
<http://www.al-anon.alateen.org/>

**Centers for Disease Control
and Prevention**
1600 Clifton Road
Atlanta, GA 30333
(800) 232- 4636
<http://www.cdc.gov/>

**National Highway Traffic Safety
Administration**
1200 New Jersey Avenue SE, West
Building
Washington, DC 20590
(888) 327-4236
<http://www.nhtsa.gov/>

**National Institute on Alcohol Abuse
and Alcoholism (NIAAA)**
Publications Distribution Center
PO Box 10686
Rockville, MD 20849
<http://www.niaaa.nih.gov/>

**Secular Organizations for Sobriety
(SOS)**
4773 Hollywood Boulevard
Hollywood, CA 90027
(323) 666-4295
**<http://www.cfiwest.org/sos/index.
htm>**

SMART Recovery
7304 Mentor Avenue, Suite F
Mentor, OH 44060
(866) 951-5357
<http://www.smartrecovery.org/>

Further Reading

Bestor, Sheri Mabry. *Substance Abuse: The Ultimate Teen Guide.* Lanham, Maryland: Scarecrow Press, 2013.

Conti, Nicolette P. and Paula Johanson. *The Truth About Amphetamines and Stimulants.* New York: Rosen Publishing Group, 2011

DiConsiglio, John. *True Confessions: Real Stories About Drinking and Drugs.* New York: Children's Press, 2008.

Edelfield, Bruce and Tracey J. Moosa. *Drug Abuse.* New York: Rosen Publishing Group, 2011

Kuhn, Cynthia, Scott Swartzwelder, and Wilkie Wilson. *Buzzed: The Straight Facts About the Most Used and Abused Drugs from Alcohol to Ecstasy.* New York: W. W. Norton & Company, 2014.

Nelson, David. *Teen Drug Abuse.* Farmington Hills, Michigan: Greenhaven Press, 2010.

Rodger, Marguerite. *Party and Club Drugs.* New York: Crabtree Publishing Company, 2011.

Sheff, Nic. *Tweak: Growing Up on Methamphetamines.* New York: Atheneum Books for Young Readers, 2009

Internet Addresses

Above the Influence.

<http://www.abovetheinfluence.com/>

National Institute on Drug Abuse. NIDA for Teens. 2013.

<http://teens.drugabuse.gov/>

TeensHealth. Drugs: What You Should Know.

<http://kidshealth.org/teen/drug_alcohol/drugs/know_about_drugs.html>

Index

M

MacPhee, Heather, 13, 60
marijuana, 55, 90
Melanie, 55–58
mental health disorders, 77
methamphetamine. *See* crystal meth
microdots, 73
Mitchell, Nick, 79

N

Narcotics Anonymous, 88
National Alcoholism and Substance
Abuse Information Center
(NASAIC), 88
neurotransmitters, 23–26
norepinephrine, 23

O

oxycodone, 90

P

pain relievers, 90
peer pressure, 10
penalties, 65, 72–73, 87
pseudoephedrine, 45

R

Reid, Samantha, 55–58, 60
resources, 88
Rohypnol
    addiction, 68–69
    adverse effects, 64
    detection of, 64, 66
    effects, 64
    first aid, 66–68
    history, 60
    identification of, 64
    manufacture, 61
    overview, 13, 60

street names, 67
uses of, 61
withdrawal, 68–69

S

serotonin, 23–26
sexual assault, 42, 61, 64–66, 68
Simons, Joe, 8, 17–19, 21
spiritual awakenings, 77
stimulants, 34
street names, 38, 53, 67, 73, 78
Substance Abuse and Mental
Health Services Administration
(SAMHSA), 88

W

windowpanes, 73